GOD'S

Blueprint

FOR

Eternal Life

John 3:16

Ben Coblentz

Other books by author:

Born To Love
Our Beautiful Heritage

Cover design and layout: Kristi Yoder

Sixth printing 2019

Printed in China

Published by:
TGS International
P.O. Box 355
Berlin, Ohio 44610 USA
Phone: 330·893·4828
Fax: 330·893·2305

TGS001848

Acknowledgements
and
A Note of Thanks

"Thank You" to the many who have become partners in writing this book by sharing thoughts, giving encouragement, and taking time to review. Special appreciation is given to Simon Schrock and David Sommers on these points; and to the many who have given encouragement and been an influence in some way or other.

Thank you and God Bless You!
Ben Coblentz

Acknowledgments

Acknowledgments Name

Table of Contents

1. For God—*The Greatest Being*

God the Father
The Father of the Universe
He is the Most High God
There is none like Him
He is the greatest Being
He is "the Only Wise God our Savior"
unto Him "be glory and majesty,
dominion and power,
both now and ever." Jude v. 25

He is the God of Creation
"In the beginning God
created the heaven and the earth." Genesis 1:1
"Of old thou hast laid the foundations of the earth:
and the heavens are the works of thy hands." Psalm 102:25
"He stretcheth out the north over the empty place,
and hangeth the earth upon nothing." Job 26:7
"Through faith we understand that the worlds
were framed by the word of God,
so that the things which are seen
were not made of things which do appear." Hebrews 11:3

God is our Creator
God made us
"Know ye not that the Lord He is God:
it is He that hath made us,
and not we ourselves;
we are His people,
and the sheep of His pasture." Psalm 100:3

God is Eternal
God came to Moses in the burning bush, saying
"I AM THAT I AM" Exodus 3:14
His existence always was and will be forever.
Our minds cannot fully comprehend such statements
because He is so much greater than our little minds.

God is Omnipresent Psalm 139:7-12
God's presence is everywhere
Darkness and light are the same to Him
We cannot get away from God
Every place we go God is there.

God is Omniscient Psalm 139:1-6
God is Infinite
God has infinite knowledge
He knows all things
"Thou knoweth my downsitting and mine uprising,
thou understandeth my thoughts afar off." Psalm 139:2
He knows our thoughts, attitudes, ambitions, and goals
He knows the intimate desires of my heart
Neither can we hide our sins from Him.

God is Omnipotent
God is all powerful and almighty
"I know that thou canst do everything,
and that no thought can be withholden thee." Job 42:2
Jesus said "With men this is impossible;
but with God all things are possible." Matthew 19:26
"Now unto Him that is able
to do exceeding abundantly

above all that we ask or think,
according to the power that worketh in us,
unto Him be glory in the church
by Christ Jesus throughout all ages." Ephesians 3:20, 21

God is all wise
"O the depths of the riches
both of the wisdom and knowledge of God!
How unsearchable are His judgments,
and His ways past finding out." Romans 11:33
"In whom are hid all the treasures
of wisdom and knowledge." Colossians 2:3
His ways and works are unsearchable.

God is a Holy God
He does not sin,
He does everything in truth and righteousness.

God is Sovereign
He has the right to do as He pleases,
He has all authority,
because He is the God of the Universe.
"Blessed be the name of God forever and ever:
for wisdom and might are His." Daniel 2:20
"None can stay His hand,
or say unto Him,
What doest thou?" Daniel 4:35

God is more than this
The heaven of heavens cannot contain Him
but He dwells in the hearts of people.

Here I caught myself trying to describe God
Forgive me, Readers, for my inability,
I can only go so far.
I am not able to explain God in His fullness,
He is so great—so good—so wonderful
so far beyond my imaginations.
God says,
"For as the heavens are higher than the earth
so are my ways higher than your ways,
and my thoughts than your thoughts." Isaiah 55:9

You look to God and ask Him
to unfold Himself to you;
God is a revelation,
I want you to experience God yourself.
God has to do it, I am not able
but God can make Himself precious to you.

God is a God of Grace
A God of Mercy
A God of Compassion
"God is Love." 1 John 4:8,16

2. So Loved—*The Greatest Choice*

Creating our solar system
and hanging it upon nothing
in that empty space in the north
was all done to make a home for mankind.
It was no accident,
It did not just happen.
God planned it so
He chose to do it
because He favors mankind.

In Genesis 1:2
"The earth was without form and void."
But God took the earth
and made a useful planet out of it.
He put light on it,
He divided the waters,
He added the sun and the moon,
He made it produce vegetation.
He created many land animals and sea creatures
and made homes for them.
God pronounced it "Good."
Last of all God created mankind.
The Bible says how He did it;
"God formed man out of the dust of the ground,
and breathed into his nostrils the breath of life;
and man became a living soul." Genesis 2:7
By this time God pronounced His creation "Very Good"
In all creation man was His noblest feature.

The basic reason for planet earth
was to create the human race
and a beautiful home for His people
where all their needs and wants are supplied.
He wanted man to multiply
and be creatures with whom
He could communicate and fellowship.
The main reason for the creation of the earth
was a vast multitude of people
which could be called His very own
and be one with them through all eternity.

It was God's choice
Love dominated the motive behind the whole scene.
Love is active.
Love makes a big difference in our lives.
Love makes us do things
we otherwise would never think of doing.
Love makes us share our best.
It seeks expression,
and it creates a sweet influence around us.

May I say again
"It was no accident."
God planned it so,
He chose to do it
For God—so loved—the world.

3. The World—*The Greatest Delinquency*

In the beautiful Garden of Eden
Adam and Eve were enjoying a perfect environment.
They were created to live forever.
Everything around them was beautiful and perfect.
They had communion and sweet fellowship with God.
Adam and Eve were allowed to
"eat of every tree in the garden
except the tree of knowledge of good and evil"
which was in the middle of the garden.

Satan came from somewhere to Eve
in the form of a serpent
and asked her enticing questions.
The serpent asked "Did God say
that you shall not eat of every tree in the garden?"
Eve answered
"We may eat of the fruit of the trees in the garden,
but God said
the fruit from the tree in the midst of the garden
we shall not eat of it,
and not even touch it lest we die."
The serpent quickly told Eve
"You shall not surely die,
for God knows that in the day you eat of it,
your eyes shall be opened
and you shall be as gods knowing good and evil." Genesis 3
The beast persuaded Eve.
Satan made it appear as if God is a liar
and withholding good from them.
It seemed as if God is not fair to them.

Eve got excited about that special tree
in the middle of the garden.
She could not get her mind and eyes off that tree.
It looked so good to eat.
It was beautiful and pleasant to the eyes.
It had the potential of wisdom built right into it.
Being fully persuaded Eve touched a fruit,
She touched it harder and pulled one off,
She bit into it and ate of it.
She gave to her husband who was with her and he ate also.

As soon as the act was committed
their eyes were opened.
They immediately saw that what they had done was evil.
They were deceived and disobedient to God.
Eating was sin because they disobeyed God.
By this time they knew who was in authority.
They appeared naked because their glory had faded.
They fell from their God created glory
to the lowest ebb of sinfulness.

Adam and Eve were obedient to Satan
He had conquered their hearts;
They had chosen lustful and proud living.
Right then and there they got the carnal nature.
They soon had children and they were the same.
Today, about a hundred generations later
the human race is still carnally minded.
This incident causes the human family to be delinquent.

All the people in the world
are born with this Adamic nature within us.

We lust, crave, fight and demand our rights
It is rightly called worldliness.
John says in his epistle
"Love not the world
neither the things that are in the world.
If any man love the world,
the love of the Father is not in him.
For all that is in the world,
the lust of the flesh,
the lust of the eyes,
and the pride of life,
is not of the Father,
but is of the world." 1 John 2:15,16
Do not love the world system of lust and pride;
The world system is enmity with God.
"The carnal mind is enmity against God:
for it is not subject to the law of God,
neither indeed can be.
So then they that are in the flesh
cannot please God." Romans 8:7,8

God does not love the worldly system,
but He loves all the people of the world.
God is no respecter of persons,
God loves everyone, yes, all of us.
Our text says
"For God—so loved—the world"
and what did He do about it?
He gave—His Son—to save
to supply the world's greatest need
and liberate us from this worldly system.

4. That He Gave—*The Greatest Deed*

Giving is an action word
Giving is an act.
When giving is incorporated with love
it is the greatest deed a man can do.
From God's perspective, giving is greater than getting
It is much more blessed.
"It is more blessed
to give than to receive." Acts 20:35

It is natural for man to grab whatever he can
and try to hold it as long as we can.
But I also notice that as people become more Godlike
that they also inherit God's perspective in giving.
They become more liberal and more sharing,
Their heart is melted into compassion,
They are more merciful.

Presently I am recuperating from a hospital stay
I had many visitors while at the hospital
and since I am home.
Some came with their Bibles.
They read scriptures and prayed for me.
They gave me encouragement from the source of love.
Others came with their songbooks to inspire me
with their melodious voices of hope and joy.
Still others came with bouquets of flowers
to radiate to me
some of God's wonderful beauty in creation.
Many gave greeting of cheer and goodwill.

I also met many who said "We are praying for you."
They all radiated a big glowing heart.
Through this experience I have been made keenly aware
of the uniqueness of people
expressing and radiating their big shining hearts.

Surely many of you have learned by experience that
the art of sharing in love
brings the greatest blessedness.
But all that we are able to give and share
is only secondary.
Because all that we own and possess
has already been given to us from God.
God gives more than all of us together can give.
God gives with pleasure
the greatest gift that can be given.
It makes God the Giver of Givers
and He does it with joy and delight;
because He knows that redeemed people
are appreciative and easy to love.
The proof of God's love is that He gave—

5. His Only Begotten Son—
The Greatest Credential

For God—so loved—the world
that He gave—His only begotten Son.
Peace and reconciliation with God
is the world's greatest need.
Jesus Christ came from the Ivory Palaces of Heaven
to make atonement for our sins
and bring peace and reconciliation with God.
"having made peace through the blood of His cross,
by Him to reconcile all things unto Himself . . .
and you,
that were sometime alienated and enemies
in your mind by wicked works,
yet now hath He reconciled." Colossians 1:20, 21

One of the most remarkable accounts of reconciliation
in Bible history is found in the book of Genesis.
The sons of Israel had relationship problems.
Joseph and Benjamin were Israel's pet sons.
Israel sent Joseph to the field
to see how his herdsmen brothers were faring.
But when Joseph arrived,
the envious brothers put Joseph in a pit
and sold him as a slave to the Egyptians.
They brought a false report back to their father.
In Egypt, Joseph was sold to Potiphar.
Soon he was in charge of Potiphar's house.
Potiphar's wife tempted him

with twinkling eyes and lustful words of adultery.
Joseph refused and fled from her, saying,
"How can I do this great wickedness
and sin against God?" Genesis 39:9
The woman made up a false report concerning Joseph
and lied to her husband about him.
He was put into prison with the King's prisoners.
The Lord was with Joseph and had mercy on him.
Whatever he did he prospered.
He was a well-favored and likeable fellow.
Very soon Joseph was in charge of the prisoners.
The King's chief butler and chief baker
were put into prison too.
They both had disturbing dreams that made them sad.
Joseph interpreted their dreams
and they were fulfilled as he interpreted them.
The butler was restored into the King's house
but the baker's future was ill-fated.
Joseph told the butler to remember him
when he comes back into the King's palace.
One night the King had a very unusual dream.
The King's wise men and astrologers
were not able to interpret the dream to the King.
The butler remembered his experience in the prison.
He told the King
about the fine young fellow in prison,
who had wisdom from God to interpret dreams.
Immediately the King sent for Joseph.
Joseph was made presentable to appear before the King.
The King poured out his heart to Joseph
and Joseph interpreted his dream, saying

"There will be seven years of bountiful harvesting
Followed by seven years of famine
with no sowing or harvesting."
Joseph advised the King to put someone in charge
to store the surplus grain in all Egypt.
The King appointed Joseph
to be ruler over all the land of Egypt.
He was made responsible to store and distribute grain.

During the seven plenteous years
the earth brought forth bountifully.
All surplus grain was to be stored
for use throughout the famine.
"And Joseph gathered corn as the sand of the sea,
very much,
until he left numbering;
for it was without number." Genesis 41:49

The famine reached into the land of Canaan
into Joseph's home country.
Israel and his sons heard about the plenty in Egypt.
Ten brothers journeyed into the far country for grain.
Upon arrival Joseph knew his brethren
but Joseph talked through an interpreter
so that they would not detect him as their brother.
They were asked many hard questions
and probed for being spies.
One brother was kept as a slave
while the others were sent home with grain.
They came home with many unanswered questions
But they soon had need for more grain.

They went again
taking along Benjamin as requested by Joseph
not knowing what would happen this time.
They were again hard pressed for honesty.
It was one of their problems.
Finally they confessed one to another
this is come upon us
because we have sinned against our brother.
They remembered the sorrow upon his face
when they sold him to the Egyptians.
Joseph understood their language.
He knew that their hearts were soft and broken.
Joseph could not hold himself any longer,
He wept aloud and said to his brothers
"I am Joseph does my father yet live?"
"I am Joseph your brother
whom you sold into Egypt."
"And he fell upon Benjamin's neck,
and wept;
and Benjamin wept upon his neck
moreover he kissed all his brethren,
and wept upon them;
and after that his brethren talked to him."
"Now therefore be not grieved,
nor angry with yourselves,
that ye sold me hither:
for God did send me before you." Genesis 45:5
There were five more years of famine ahead
So the whole Israel family was welcomed to dwell
in the bountiful plains of Goshen in Egypt.

Behind the scene God was working out a plan
to reconcile the Israel family.
It took years and years of hard work and patience
storing and distributing grain
and building storehouses without number.
Many times we are blind to God's work
and don't realize His work in melting our hearts
to reconcile us to Himself and our fellowmen.

God's plan worked.
The Israel family was reconciled.
Joseph was their savior.

Joseph is a type of Jesus Christ.
The whole world needs reconciliation.
We all need to make peace with God.
Christ is God's Savior for the whole world.
We can draw salvation from Christ's credit account.
His credential has no reserves.
Enough blood was shed at Calvary to redeem every soul.
Eternal life is man's greatest gift.
May we fall upon Jesus Christ
confess Him as Savior, Lord and Master
and weep tears of repentance upon His neck.

6. That Whosoever—*The Greatest Proposal*

God seems to be telling me that we Christians
should get ready and send out at least
six billion (6,000,000,000) invitations
to invite the whole human race
to the marriage supper of the Lamb of God,
So that anyone who chooses to respond
may have a fair opportunity.
I am afraid there are millions out there
who have not yet been contacted.
One of these days the proposal period will be over,
God's harvest of people will be completed
and time will be no more.

Luke records an incident where a certain man
made a great feast and invited many people
but they excused themselves
because of business priorities.
The master then quickly sent out his servants to
invite the poor, the maimed, the halt, and the blind.
Then there was still more room
so he sent his servants out again.
They went into the highways and hedges
and compelled people to come in
so that his house might be filled.
The poor and needy responded readily.
It is always easiest to help someone who has a need.

In another occasion Matthew relates where a king
made a wedding feast for his son.

Again many guest were not worthy
so he commanded his servants
to "Go ye therefore into the highways,
and as many as ye shall find bid to the marriage." Matthew
22:9
These invitations were urgent.
It called for action right now.

God invites us to accept His gift.
"The gift of God is eternal life
through Jesus Christ our Lord." Romans 6:23
Salvation is a gift.
Salvation is not a reward for doing good.
"Not of works lest anyone should boast." Ephesians 2:9
God's plan of salvation is so beautifully designed
that no person gets any glory for the heavenly entry.
God gets all the glory and credit.
His plan is so far beyond our thinking.

If we would have designed a plan
we would probably have concluded
that the more good and struggling we do
the surer we are to get into heaven.
If we could get in with works
we would have reason to boast.
If you would boast about your good works
and I about mine
we would have a competitive spirit.
That was Satan's problem when he was in heaven.
He had the I, I, I spirit,
the better than thou attitude.

That is why he was cast out of heaven.

Luke records a parable where
"Two men went up into the temple to pray;
one a Pharisee, the other a Publican.
The Pharisee stood and prayed thus with himself,
God, I thank thee,
that I am not as other men are,
extortioners, unjust, adulterers
or even as this publican.
I fast twice in the week,
I give tithe of all that I possess.
And the Publican standing afar off
would not lift up so much as his eyes unto heaven,
but smote upon his breast, saying
God be merciful to me a sinner.
I tell you,
this man went down to his house justified
rather than the other:
for everyone that exalteth himself
shall be abased;
and he that humbleth himself
shall be exalted." Luke 18:10-14

All that the Pharisee did and said was to
praise, justify, exalt, and boast about himself.
He asked nothing, confessed nothing,
and received nothing.
But the publican saw himself as a sinner.
He came to God with a need and cried out for mercy.
The Publican was justified by God

because God heard his prayer.

We are often invited to many special occasions
weddings, dinners, graduations,
business and sales parties.
They are like an appointment.
They make life and people important.
But God's invitation makes God important.
It is the greatest proposal that ever visited mankind.
It is the most important thing in life now
because its effect reaches into all eternity.

The whosoever includes
You—me—anyone—yes everyone.
God says "Come"
You are invited
May we find ourselves
Poor in spirit
ready and willing to say
"I believe that Jesus Christ is the Son of God"
"God, I will accept your great gift to me;
your Son Jesus Christ"
"I will give room for Jesus in my heart."

7. Believeth In Him—*The Greatest Offer*

It takes faith to trust God
that Jesus is the Savior of the world, and say
"I believe that Jesus Christ is the Son of God."
It takes faith and humility to say
"God, I will accept your great gift to me;
your Son Jesus Christ."
It takes faith to give room in my heart for Jesus.
It takes faith to accept God at His word
and believe every word in the Bible.
"If thou shalt confess with thy mouth the Lord Jesus,
and shalt believe in thine heart
that God hath raised Him from the dead,
thou shalt be saved.
For with the heart man believeth unto righteousness;
and with the mouth confession
is made unto salvation." Romans 10:9, 10

An account in Numbers 21 tells
that the Israelites in the wilderness
were bitten by poisonous snakes and were dying.
These people were in desperate need
and crying out to God for help.
They wanted God to take away the fiery serpents.
God did not take away the serpents
but gave them something better.
God told Moses to make a serpent of brass
and display it on a pole
so everyone can look at it.

God promised healing to everybody
who would turn their eyes in faith
and look at the brazen serpent.
I can imagine some people were so sick
that they could not so much as lift their head
to look toward the brazen serpent
but friends and loved ones would carry them
to where they could see and be healed and live.
Great miracles took place that day!
Believing is faith in action,
They were healed because of their faith.
"As Moses lifted up the serpent in the wilderness,
even so must the Son of Man be lifted up.
That whosoever believeth in Him should not perish,
but have eternal life." John 3:14, 15
Jesus was lifted up on the cross for our salvation.

    Believing in Jesus
is the greatest opportunity of a lifetime.
Our hearts sorrow to think that there may be millions
who never get the opportunity to believe in Jesus.
They have no one to help them look to Jesus.
Many however will face the question,
like the Philippian jailor who asked
"What must I do to be saved?"
The answer was given him
"Believe on the Lord Jesus Christ,
and thou shalt be saved." Acts 16:30, 31
Paul quotes "Gospel of your salvation." Ephesians 1:13
"Wherein ye stand; by which also ye are saved"
1 Corinthians 15:1, 2

When the unsaved repent of their sins,
they are "saved" and have the assurance of heaven.
Millions have experienced this transaction,
testifying that they have in a moment,
as the Bible assures them,
"passed from death unto life" John 5:24
and from "darkness to light" Acts 26:18
And they "know" that they "have eternal life." 1 John 5:13

Some people look at Jesus as a great person.
Certain Greeks came to Christ's disciples
and said "We want to see Jesus."
They wanted to see a great man.
Jesus was not revealed to them.
He was not for show.

Another person wanted to see Jesus
It was Zaccheus.
He was a short man
and could not see Jesus because of the crowd.
He climbed up a Sycamore tree.
Jesus saw him and he saw Jesus.
Zaccheus saw Jesus as a Savior.
Zaccheus repented of his sins.
He confessed them and made restitution.
Jesus came to help people repent. Luke 19:1-10

The Good Samaritan account in Luke 10
clearly teaches us who our next door neighbors are.
The next door reaches as far

as our compassion stretches.
Looking at this parable from a spiritual view
Christ is like the Good Samaritan who journeyed the earth.
The human family is wounded with sin
and we are half dead and dying.
Jesus' compassion reaches to everyone.
Jesus invested His life, even His blood
for the injury we inherited from the Garden of Eden
and all our sins we committed.
He paid the full price for the whole human race.

The wounded man was helpless.
He accepted the Good Samaritan's help.
He could not pay him back for his compassion.
Likewise, the human race is helpless
and we cannot pay back God for all His good to us.
We can, however, show our appreciation to God
and be a kind next door neighbor
by showing compassion to the lost,
helpless, and needy people of the world.

Jesus came to give His blood for our sins
In the Old Testament sacrifice services
blood from animals were used for sin offerings.
They were types and shadows of what was coming.
Jesus Christ's blood offering at Calvary
was the perfect fulfillment
of Old Testament types and shadows.
"Not by the blood of goats and calves,
but by His own blood

He entered in once into the holy place,
having obtained eternal redemption for us." Hebrews 9:12
Through Christ's blood
    we are reconciled
    we are justified
    we are redeemed
    we are saved
    we are cleansed
    and totally forgiven
Accepting Christ's blood offering
brings peace to our conscience toward God.

May we say with the Ethiopian eunuch in Acts 8:37
"I believe that Jesus Christ is the Son of God."

8. Should Not Perish— *The Greatest Liberation*

Satan captured Eve's heart in the Garden of Eden.
She had coveted to be like the gods.
She was created to live forever
but now she had to die.
She was doomed to perish with Satan.
But God promised Eve a Savior the very same day
that the death sentence was pronounced upon her.
She recognized and claimed that promise
because when her first child was born
she already thought him to be the Savior.
But generation after generation
kept looking for the Savior for nearly 4,000 years
until finally God gave His Son
to be the Savior of the world.
"Who gave Himself for our sins,
that He might deliver us
from this present evil world." Galatians 1:4
"Whatsoever is born of God overcometh the world,
even our faith.
Who is he that overcometh the world,
but he that believeth that Jesus is the Son
of God." 1 John 5:4, 5
"Ye . . . have overcome . . .
because greater is He that is in you,
than he that is in the world." 1 John 4:4
These scriptures very vividly
point out the truth about liberation.

Our overcoming and victory is by faith
believing in Jesus the Son of God
and having Him dwelling in our hearts.
Christ in us is greater than the satanic forces
which also dwell in people.
Satan is powerful but Christ is all powerful.
"The riches of the glory of this mystery . . .
is Christ in you, the hope of glory." Colossians 1:27
Inviting Christ into your heart
gives Him the permission
to sit upon the throne of your heart
to rule and to reign there;
to gain the victory over the worldly system.

The victory is in the indwelling Christ
Receiving Christ is the gateway to victory
It gives us the power to say "No"
to the worldly standards of life
to overcome the lust of the flesh,
the lust of the eyes,
and the pride of life.
So that we can live:
a separated life unto God
a cross-bearing life
a non-resistant life
a life committed to obey the Gospel of Christ
a life yielded to uphold Bible standards and doctrine
in continued repentance
growing in faith
flourishing in charity
and waiting patiently

This is deliverance, freedom, and liberation
that will save us from perishing.

   Satan is doomed to eternal hellfire
and all those who continue in ungodly
wicked and immoral living
will share punishment with Satan.
Missing out on deliverance
and liberation in this life
also cancels out eternal bliss
in the eternity ahead.
God's program is instituted—
first—
to deliver us from this present evil world
and secondly—
to save us from the wrath
of God's eternal damnation.
This is the greatest deliverance
that was ever offered to mankind.

9. But Have Everlasting Life—
The Greatest Delight

To claim the promise of everlasting life
brings great joy into our hearts.
"Restore unto me the joy of thy salvation" Psalm 51:12
"With joy shall ye draw water
from the wells of salvation." Isaiah 12:3
There is great joy in assurance of salvation.
Throughout scriptures we see men and women
yes, great multitudes rejoicing.
To name a few—the Apostles, the assembly on Pentecost,
and thousands in the early church and missionaries.
Surely many sowed in tears,
in sorrows, trials, and tribulations
but deep inside there was an abounding joy.
Many of the martyrs
throughout the history of the church
went to the stake with joy
singing and praising God to be counted worthy
to suffer for the Lord Jesus Christ.
In reviewing church history,
we notice that the more who were killed for their faith
the more were added to the faith in Christ
because of their radiant testimony
and their evident joy in the Lord.
They could face it with joy because they claimed
the promises of God's word
with assurance and confidence.
"Thy word was unto me the joy
and rejoicing of my heart:
for I am called by thy name." Jeremiah 15:16

"I will rejoice in the Lord,
I will joy in the God of my salvation." Habakkuk 3:18
"And not only so, but we also joy in God
through our Lord Jesus Christ
by whom we have now received
the atonement." Romans 5:11
"Delight thyself also in the Lord:
and He shall give thee the desires of thine heart." Psalm 37:4
Christ came from heaven and it is His delight
to fill us with Holy Spirit joy.
"that your joy may be full." John 15:11

    "Blessed are they that mourn
for they shall be comforted." Matthew 5:4
Our past life may have been a mess
and we may be ever so sorry
but there is oil of joy for those who mourn
and come to Christ for forgiveness which brings
"joy unspeakable and full of glory." 1 Peter 1:8
"There is joy in the presence of the angels of God
over one sinner that repenteth." Luke 15:10
The Angel that announced Christ's birth said
"I bring you good tidings of great joy,
which shall be to all people." Luke 2:10
Receiving salvation in Jesus Christ brings us
"the joy of the Holy Ghost." 1 Thessalonians 1:6
"Joy" is a fruit of the Spirit. Galatians 5:22
These scriptures plainly teach us
that joy is experienced in this life.
It is a joy that comforts.
A joy that brings fulfillment in life.
A joy unspeakable and full of glory.

It overflows the heart and radiates to others.

Our joy is firmly rooted
in the hope of eternal life.
We are committed
"Unto Him that is able to keep us from falling,
and to present us faultless,
before the presence of His glory
with exceeding joy." Jude v. 24
We have great reason to believe that the eternal joys
far exceed anything that we know now.
"The sufferings of this present time
are not worthy to be compared with the glory
which shall be revealed in us." Romans 8:18
"In thy presence is fulness of joy;
at thy right hand
there are pleasures forever more." Psalm 16:11
In the parable of the talents Jesus said
that the faithful shall hear the blessed words
"enter thou into the joy of the Lord." Matthew 25:21,23
What a joy that will be
to live in the Holy City
coming out of heaven
adorned as a bride for her husband
with pearly gates
and streets of gold.
Where everyone is radiating with joy
praising and adoring the Lord
whose glory is a Holy Presence
—forever—
Our benefit of this whole program
is everlasting "JOY"!

10. John 3:16—*The Greatest Plan*

"For God so loved the world
that He gave His only begotten Son
that whosoever believeth in Him
should not perish but have everlasting life."
John 3:16 is considered by many
as the greatest scripture verse in the Bible.
I would like to say there are many great
and wonderful scriptures throughout the Bible
and that this verse is a very great quote
in the Greatest Book the Holy Bible.
It describes God's plan to save man.
It is the blueprint for eternal life.
It is the most important subject in life
because its effects reach far beyond this life.

The main character in the scriptures is God.
He is "the Only Wise God our Savior" Jude v. 25
He is the greatest Being.
In the whole Bible,
God is never a questionable issue
God is eternal
God is holy
God is sovereign
    almighty
    all knowing
    everywhere present
    all wise
"God is love" 1 John 4:8, 16
He is the Creator.

Man was His noblest feature in all creation.
Love dominated His action.
He did it because He knew that redeemed people
would be very appreciative and easy to love.

    After Adam and Eve sinned in the Garden
and the sting of Satan was sore
God gave them another chance.
He designed a plan to buy us back
to reconcile us
to redeem us
to negotiate peace with us
and cancel the debt.
It was God's choice,
He made the move,
God planned it.
He chose to save the world with grace.
We have the greatest need,
the greatest want,
the greatest lack,
We have a great debt load.
Our sins are a debt load
which we are never able to pay,
not even in a whole lifetime.
The human race is delinquent.

    Therefore God gave
It is the greatest deed.
He gave His son Jesus Christ.
His life and sacrifice is for our credential.
Our sins may be charged to Christ's account.

Jesus paid a debt load which He did not owe.
"He was bruised for our iniquities:
and with His stripes we are healed.
And the Lord hath laid on Him
the iniquity of us all." Isaiah 53:5,6
Only by the blood of Jesus do we find forgiveness
Our good works and boasting produces no credit.
The beauty of God's plan is
we are all on one level
SAVED BY GRACE
and God gets all the glory.

The greatest proposal invites
you—me—whosoever
to the greatest offer to mankind
to believe in Jesus Christ
and escape the power of the evil forces.
To liberate us and give us freedom
to practice holy living in this life
so that we can look forward with great delight
and joy to everlasting bliss.

God has made a great investment in the human race
and the price is paid to buy us back.
John 3:16 unveils God's plan.
It is God's blueprint to save fallen man.
May we through the impulse of love
respond to the privilege to become sons of God
and inherit the eternal promises.
Our benefit in total commitment
is everlasting life.

11. A Sinner's Prayer

(A sample of what may be prayed)

Thank you Father in Heaven
for showing your love to me.
I want to repent
I want to have peace and be reconciled to you
God be merciful to me a sinner.
I believe that Jesus Christ is the Son of God
and that He died for me at Calvary
to atone for my sins,
my inherited sin
and the sins that I have committed.
I confess that I am a sinner by nature
I have sinned against you.
(Continue to confess as led by the Spirit of God)

Cover my sin and my sins with the blood of Jesus
and forgive them in Jesus' name.
Thank you,
I accept Jesus as my Savior, Lord and Master
Let Him come on the throne of my heart
and help me say "No" to sins
so that I can live a holy life
a separated life unto you
a cross-bearing life
a non-resistant life
a life obedient to your Gospel.
I want to be committed to live Bible doctrine.
I do not want to miss heaven.
I want to enjoy heaven with the redeemed.
Thank you Holy Father
in the Name of Jesus.